My First Book about the Alphabet of Nocturnal Animals

Amazing Animal Books Children's Picture Books

By Molly Davidson

Mendon Cottage Books

JD-Biz Publishing

Read More Amazing Animal Books

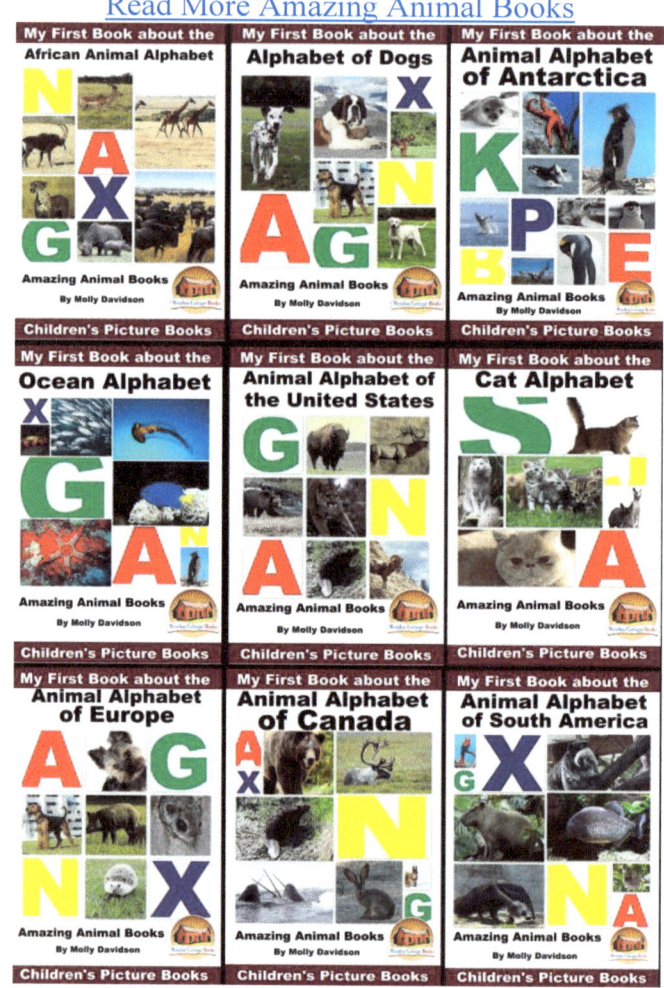

Purchase at Amazon.com

Download Free Books!

http://MendonCottageBooks.com

Introduction

Nocturnal animals are mostly active at night and sleep or are less active during the day.

One of the main reasons many animals choose to be active at night, is to avoid predators that may try to attack during the day.

 **is for an Anaconda.**

Anacondas are the largest snakes in the World; they live in the tropical swamps of South America.

They hunt at night, and will squeeze, or constrict, their prey until they die.

 **is for a Badger.**

They can be seen in many habitats throughout Asia, Europe, and North America.

Badgers dig burrows, large holes, in the dirt, which is where they live.

They hunt at night for frogs, snakes, worms, insects, and rodents, many times digging into the dirt to get their prey.

C is for a Caiman.

Caiman live in streams, rivers, and lakes in the tropical rainforest of South America.

They spend most of the day in the water, and will hunt at night, for fish, birds, reptiles, and turtles, which they swallow whole.

D is for a Dingo.

Dingoes are a wild dog found on the dry plains of Australia.

Since it is so warm during the day, they hunt kangaroos, rats, lizards, rabbits, and birds, at night when it is cooler.

E is for an Erinaceinae, the scientific name for a Hedgehog.

They are found in the wild in Africa, Asia, Europe, and New Zealand.

Hedgehogs have stiff, spiky snipes on the top of their bodies, for protection from predators.

 **is for a Fruit Bat.**

Fruit bats live in the forests of Asia, Africa, Europe, and Australia; where they fly around eating various fruits at night.

G is for a Great Horned Owl.

The Great Horned Owl sees mostly in black and white which helps them hunt for rodents, fish, and small animals at night.

 **is for a Hamster.**

Hamsters in the wild live in burrows during the day, and then they come out at night to eat.

They have bad eye-sight so they use smell to find their food and their way around.

They are a very popular pet around the World.

 **is for a Jaguar.**

Jaguars are wild cats that live in forests in Central and South America.

They hunt alligators, birds, monkeys, reptiles, and turtles at night; where they may bury their prey so they can come eat more later.

K is for a Kiwi.

Kiwi birds cannot fly and they live in New Zealand, but are becoming extinct.

They use their long beaks to hunt at night for worms, insects, and spiders.

L is for a Lemur.

Lemurs live in families of around 15, high in the trees on the island of Madagascar.

They have long tails, like their monkey relatives.

They look for food, which is mostly seeds, nuts, or fruit, during the cool night hours.

L is also for a Lobster.

Lobsters have a tough shell which helps protect them from predators on the ocean floor.

They are active at night, where they search for food, such as crabs, clams, worms, snails, flounder fish, and mussels.

M is for a Millipede.

The word millipede means 1,000 legs, but they actually only have between 47 - 197 legs.

Millipedes like to eat dead or decaying plants in the cool night air.

When they are in danger they roll into a ball to protect their soft under bellies.

 **is for a Nurse Shark.**

Nurse sharks live on the bottom of tropical oceans, usually in the coral reef.

At night they hunt for squid, lobsters, fish, octopus, and crustaceans living on the ocean floor.

O

is for an Okapi.

Okapi, also called forest giraffes, live in the Congo River Basin in Africa.

They have a long, sticky tongue which helps them reach leaves and plants, which they eat at night.

P is for a Pangolin.

Pangolin, also called scaly anteaters, live in the grasslands of Africa and Southeast Asia.

It has not teeth so it will use its long, sticky tongue at night to catch ants, termites, and other insects.

 is for a Quoll.

Quoll are a small marsupial found in the grasslands and rainforests of Tasmania.

They live in burrows during the day, and at night they go in search of food, which may include insects, fruit, rabbits, mice, and rats.

R is for a Red-Eyed Tree Frog.

Red -Eyed Tree Frogs live in the rainforests of Central and South America.

They sleep under the shade of leaves during the day and use their long, sticky tongues to catch insects at night.

S is for a Snapping Turtle.

Snapping turtles live in freshwater ponds, streams, and canals in eastern North America.

They spend most of their time in the water; they hunt at night for snakes, frogs, small fish, and insects.

T is for a Three Toed Sloth.

Three Toed Sloths spend most of their life hanging upside down in the trees of the rainforest in Central and South America.

They spend about 15 hours per day sleeping and are active at night.

T is also for a Tuatara.

Tuataras are reptiles that only live on the islands surrounding New Zealand.

They have a third eye on the top of their forehead.

They hunt for food in the cool night air.

U

is for a Ursus Arctos, the scientific name for a Grizzly Bear.

Grizzly bears live in cooler mountains and river valleys.

They are most active at night, and can run up to 35 mph.

V  is for a Vinegaroon.

Vinegaroons are scorpions that live in the deserts of the southern U.S. and Mexico.

They hide under rocks and leaves to stay cool during the day, and use their large pinchers to catch prey at night.

W

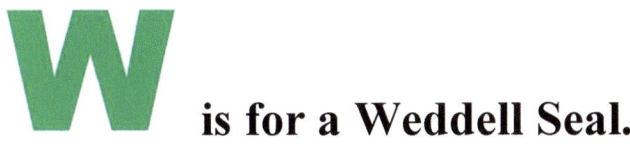 is for a Weddell Seal.

Weddell seals live on the coastal ice in Antarctica.

They do most of their hunting in the ocean water at night; this helps them avoid many predators.

 **is also for a White Tailed Deer.**

White Tailed Deer live in meadows close to forests from southern Canada to northern South America.

They use their white tails to sign others that there is danger.

Z is for a Zorilla.

The Zorilla is a skunk looking weasel, which lives on the African savannas.

They have scent glands under their tail which they use to spray a strong smelling liquid when threatened.

Zorilla dig burrows to live in during the hot days, and they hunt for insects, birds, and reptiles at night.

Conclusion

I hope you have enjoying reading about amazing nocturnal animals.

One more fact, the air is still at night, so scents stay in the air longer, making it easier for nocturnal animals to find food.

Download Free Books!

http://MendonCottageBooks.com

Our books are available at

1. Amazon.com

2. Barnes and Noble

3. Itunes

4. Kobo

5. Smashwords

6. Google Play Books

Download Free Books!
http://MendonCottageBooks.com

Publisher

JD-Biz Corp

P O Box 374

Mendon, Utah 84325

http://www.jd-biz.com/

www.ingramcontent.com/pod-product-compliance
Lightning Source LLC
Chambersburg PA
CBHW050902290526
45792CB00002B/676